The
GROUNDINGS
EXPERIENCE
LEADERS GUIDE

THE
GROUNDINGS
EXPERIENCE
LEADER'S GUIDE

Candie Blankman

BVB

Bold Vision Books
PO Box 2011
Friendswood, Texas 7749

TABLE OF CONTENTS

FOR *GROUNDINGS* LEADERS

Welcome to a journey you will be on for the rest of your life!

Grounded in Christ means paying attention to what God is doing in you and the world around you and to how Jesus might be inviting you to participate. As a leader, you will be taking others along with you. May God bless you and build His Kingdom through you and those you lead.

In order to assist you with the Bible study portion of *Groundings* the following is included in this Leader's Manual:

1. "Leader only notes."

2. There is some "background information" before each text.

3. The "Basic Facts" for each text are listed before the text.

4. The answers to "Questions About the Facts" are included after each question.

5. Familiarize yourself with these before each session.

In order to maximize the time you have together in each *Groundings* session:

1. When sharing personal stories have participants summarize and write their stories in a few sentences before they share with the group. This encourages focus and prevents rambling.

2. The recommended time flow of each session has been estimated based on the experience of many groups. Whenever you have more than 6 people in the experience, break up into small groups (dyads or triads) in order to maximize more participation. Then if time allows have each of the small groups report a summary or MAIN learning back to the larger group. It is the responsibility of the leader to watch the time and guide participants in the use of time.

3. When praying, both to save time and assist those who are not used to praying out loud, give out 3x5 cards with "fill in the blank" prayer suggestions. I.e. "Lord, help _____ to see who it is that you want me to listen to and talk to." Or write questions on 3x5 cards that help to identify prayer needs, i.e. "What is it that is most challenging to you in *Groundings* right now?" or "Who is the person or what is the setting where it is most difficult for you to _____?" or "What is the greatest obstacle to your doing this assignment this week?"

In order to model what you teach:

1. Be attentive to what God is doing in the session you are in. If there is an "aha" moment with a participant or if you as the leader sense something significant happening in a group, stop and name it, and to the degree that it is appropriate, talk about it, then give thanks for it.

2. Do the homework and be prepared to give very brief examples to encourage others, even if it is a "failed" example. This, too, will encourage students to keep trying.

In order to maximize accountability for living the experience and to encourage full commitment, set up some way for the group to stay connected between sessions.

1. Prayer partners that will call each other between sessions and find out how they can pray for each other.

2. Journal sharing—pair participants to call and share a learning from their journal between each session.

3. Set up a Facebook page or email group so that members of the experience can check in whenever they are able to see what others are doing and where they can ask for help with a challenge they are having or share excitement about an encounter.

WHY GROUNDINGS?

This curriculum was developed to help anyone who desires to follow Christ (be a disciple) more faithfully. It is designed to help Christians encounter Jesus alive in the stories and teaching of the New Testament and to discover where each of us are found in those stories and teachings. The material was birthed out of everyday congregational life where it is common for us to take classes on discipleship and to have a great deal of knowledge *about* the Bible and Jesus. And yet, it seems uncommon for us to be actively engaged in living out and sharing our experience of Jesus in every day places and every day ways—like Jesus did!

Groundings is about being grounded in the living Christ by knowing our own faith stories, noticing God at work in ourselves and others, and opening ourselves up to being part of what God is doing in and around and through us every day.

In *Groundings* we like to say that Christ is present and powerfully at work in every square inch of the universe writing the Kingdom story. The only difference is whether we notice it and whether or not we offer our story to be a part of the bigger story of God's Kingdom work in the world.

Consequently, *Groundings* is designed as an experience to be lived not a class to take. It will challenge all who engage the material to make discipleship an everyday moment by moment experience. And it will challenge all who participate to make discipleship and evangelism a seamless garment. Living in and proclaiming Christ are the same exercise.

As we open ourselves to studying the Scripture to encounter the living Christ and to see ourselves in relation to him, we are opened to the power of experiencing Christ and allowing others to see and hear that experience. But we are also humbled to see and hear Christ at work in others—at times in people and places where we might least expect it. This is the transformation of a worldview and *Groundings* is designed to help facilitate this transformation.

HOW?
SIX GATHERINGS

This material is designed to be experienced in six sessions or gatherings. The first five sessions require two hours each followed by *at least* two weeks in between each session to observe the *Groundings* principles in life and to complete the assignments. This time allows participants to live out the experience. Then participants return to the next session to report and share their discoveries of Christ at work in and around them and their responses to those experiences.

The final session is longer, three to five hours, and is designed as a mini retreat where participants explore and discern how they might pass this experience on to others.

Groundings can be done with a large group that is broken up into smaller groups of 4-6 during the gatherings. It can be experienced in one small group of 4-8, or in dyads or triads. In any case it requires a person to facilitate who has already completed the experience or spent time preparing carefully. Resources for training leaders are available at www.candieblankman.com. But as we have now learned from years of *Groundings*, every time someone facilitates this experience, they continue to encounter the living Christ and become a participant every bit as much as a facilitator.

Experiencing the living Christ

always transforms a person.

GROUNDINGS OVERVIEW

OVERVIEW

Seven main components (*) make up *The Groundings Experience*

*Lectio Divina: May be done one step each week or all steps every week depending on how much experience the group has had with lectio divina. See Appendix I for definitions and instructions.

    Session 1 – Silence/Read/Listen
    Session 2 – Reflect
    Session 3 – Respond
    Session 4 – Contemplate
    Session 5 – Resolve
    Session 6 – Putting them all together

*Modules: Session 1 through Session 6

    Session 1: Proclaiming the Kingdom – Mary annoints Jesus
        (Matthew 26 and Luke 7)
    Session 2: Noticing God at Work – The Woman at the Well
        (John 4)
    Session 3: Listening to our Neighbors – The Good Samaritan
        (Luke 10)
    Session 4: Giving and Receiving Hospitality - Zacchaeus
        (Luke 19)

Session 5: Understanding the Mission of God – Nicodemus
    (John 3)
Session 6: Groundings: What's Next? (a "mini-retreat")

*Prayer:
For and with each other
For the people we will encounter

*Encountering Jesus in the Scripture.

*Small and Large Group Work:
- Looking at Scripture with new and fresh lenses and open hearts

- Learning to ask questions about the text and discovering yourself in the story

- Learning to focus when we listen and when we speak

- Inviting others to speak

- Learning to ask good questions that invite others to open up

*Journaling:
Writing and drawing and cutting and pasting as often as possible about *The Groundings Experience* during and between the six gatherings

*Assignments Together and Alone:
- Taking risks by engaging with people in our everyday contexts who are new to us or new to having conversations with us about faith and God at work in the world and recording as much as possible (journaling)

- Asking questions more than giving answers, listening more than talking, being transparent about successes and failures in living out this experience when we report back to the *Groundings* group

A Covenant for Participants

Together in *Groundings*, through prayer, Bible study, and discussion

I will take Jesus at His word and put those words into action at home, work, school, and play.

I will learn new ways, affirm some old ways, and undo unhelpful ways of following Jesus by taking a fresh look at His teaching and His life. With God's help.

I will covenant to be transparent and vulnerable in honestly doing my assignments and sharing my daily experiences of following Jesus into the world, for the sake of the world, and for the sake of my Christian community.

I will pray for the group.

I will help others in my *Groundings Experience* and allow them to help me in discerning where and how to teach others how to become grounded in Jesus and offering themselves to work in his Kingdom through *The Groundings Experience*.

Signed   _____

Date   _____

GROUNDINGS

Session 1

PROCLAIMING THE KINGDOM

MATTHEW 26:6-13, LUKE 7:36-50

Pass out participants manual.

Turning Event 20 minutes

Share (in pairs or whole table group) in **two minutes** about the event/time in your life when you turned the corner from just believing **about** Jesus to **wanting to follow** Jesus. Then one person from each table (if multiple tables) share (with permission) with the larger group, the one experience of another person that inspired/surprised them.

You will be facilitating lectio divina *before* you do the overview of *Groundings*. This is intentional. The greatest obstacle to encountering the living Christ is thinking we already know "what the Bible says." This exercise reveals this in full living color! Even if participants really struggle with lectio, it helps prepare them to open up to old stories with new eyes and ears.

Give the overview of lectio divina below in your own words as much as possible. For more information, read the book, *Sacred Rythms, pages 61-64* by Ruth Haley Barton. A more expanded explanation of lectio for *Groundings* is found in Appendix I. Be sure to study this carefully before you begin to facilitate lectio.

Beginning

Choose a passage (six to eight verses); it can be part of your normal reading plan, a passage you select for today or a passage from the lectionary reading for this week. There are several passages already printed out in the Appendix II. Whatever passage you choose, enter prayerfully into the lectio process. Following are very detailed instructions to help you learn the moves. You will need to survey the group to find out how experienced they are with lectio. More experienced groups can do several or all the steps the first time. Less experienced groups will need to move more slowly. For the sake of those new to lectio you will only teach one part of lectio each week, except for the first week you will do silencio and lectio. Each session you will add another one of the lectio steps so that by the fifth session participants will be doing a full lectio exercise.

Preparation (Silencio)

Take a moment to come fully into the present. With your eyes closed, let your body relax, and allow yourself to become consciously aware of God's presence with you. Express your willingness (or your willingness to be made willing) to hear from God in these moments by using a brief prayer such as "Come Lord Jesus," or "Here I am," or "Speak, Lord, for your servant is listening."

Read (Lectio)

Listen for the word or the phrase that is addressed to you. Turn to the passage and begin to read slowly, pausing between phrases and sentences. You may read silently, or you may find it helpful to read the passage aloud, allowing the words to echo and resonate, sink in and settle into your heart. As you read, listen for a word or phrase that strikes you or catches your attention. Allow a moment of silence, repeating that word or phrase softly to yourself, pondering it and savoring it as though pondering the words of a loved one. This is the word that is meant for you. Be content to listen simply and openly, without judging or analyzing.

Reflect (Meditatio)

How is my life touched by this word? Once you have heard the word that is meant for you, read the passage again, and listen for the way this passage connects with your life. Ask, what is it in my life right now that needs to hear this word? Allow several moments of silence following this reading, and explore thoughts, perceptions and sensory impressions. If the passage is a story, perhaps ask yourself, where am I in this scene? What do I hear as I imagine myself in the story or hear these words addressed specifically to me? How do the dynamics of this story connect with my own life experience?

Respond (Oratio)

What is my response to God based on what I have read and encountered? Read the passage one more time, listening for your own deepest and truest response. In silence after the reading, allow your prayer to flow spontaneously from your heart as fully and as truly as you can. At this point you are entering into a personal dialogue with God. Pay attention to any sense that God is inviting you to act or to respond in some way to the word you have heard. You may find it helpful to write your prayers or to journal at this point.

Rest (Contemplatio)

Rest in the Word of God. In this final reading you are invited to release and return to a place of rest in God. You have given your response its full expression, so now you can move into a time of waiting and resting in God's presence, like the weaned child who leans against its mother (Psalm 131:2). This is a posture of total yieldedness and abandon to the great Lover of your soul.

Resolve (Incarnatio)

Incarnate (live out) the Word of God. As you emerge from this place of personal encounter with God to life in the company of others, resolve to carry this word with you and to live it out in the context of daily life and activity. As you continue to listen to the word throughout the day, you will be led deeper and deeper into its meaning, until it begins to live in you and you enflesh this word to the world in which you live. As a way of supporting your intent to live out the word you have been given, you may want to choose an image, a picture or a symbol that you can carry to remind you of it.

Lectio Divina   20 minutes

There is an important distinction between a "taking it apart" mentality versus a "the text speaking to me" (taking me apart).

Lectio divina is listening not analyzing.

Lectio divina is a practice that must be cultivated.

Lectio divina does not happen easily or quickly.

Like learning to distinguish bird songs, you must be able to eliminate competing songs and sounds in order to hear a particular song. So, too, we must practice and learn to eliminate all sorts of voices and thoughts in order to learn to hear God speaking through the text.

Lectio divina is all about reading/listening with no agenda. It is about a relationship with the living Christ revealing himself through the text.

Lectio divina is paying attention to how I feel/what I think hearing this text.

Silence/Read/Listen

Colossians 1:15-20 (or other text)

Texts are in the participant's manual in Appendix II. If you have selected a different passage have copies of a text you want to use for participants.

- Identify three different readers.
- Take 30 seconds of silence to prepare, focus, put aside distractions. (Silence or *Silencio)*
- Listen as each reader reads the text slowly.
- Be silent 30 seconds to 1 minute in between each reading.

1. When three readings and silence are complete, share anything that made it hard to listen and hear.

2. What are you thinking about?

3. What distracts you?

4. What is your attitude at this very time toward lectio divina? (Be honest.)

5. Share a word or phrase that stood out, but do not explain why.

If your group has had more experience with lectio divina, you will move through the texts more quickly. As the facilitator, you will discern how fast to move with your group.

Use the following to give an overview of *The Groundings Experience*

Introduction to *Groundings* | 20 minutes |

Challenge: Look at these texts and the life and teaching of Jesus with fresh eyes and open hearts, not to simply repeat what we already know or have always thought.

Vision: See how being grounded in Christ in everyday life also opens up our lives to seeing God at work all around us, living the Good News, and sharing it with others in a very comfortable and natural way.

Commitment: Make attendance a priority and do the assignments with whole heart and mind. Everyone signs the Covenant. *pg 17 in participants.*

Respect: We share the time we have together so that all participants have equal opportunity to speak. Each participant takes responsibility for their level of participation.

Journal: Draw or write in a journal the key elements of a particular experience in and out of session for deeper processing and fuller sharing with the group (not attempting to remember or speak extemporaneously). A journal is provided in the *Groundings* Kit.

Lectio: Different people have different levels of experience with lectio divina. Please commit to trying and participating and opening up to what God might want to do in and through you through this way of reading/listening to Scripture.

Confidentiality: *The Groundings Experience* as a whole is fully intended to be shared. You are free to share your experience with anyone. However, we will respect and not repeat any stories or experiences of others without the express permission of the individual. We are entering holy ground.

Define: We will be using the term "third space." A "third space" is any place where we begin to see and experience as a place where God is present and at work. I.e. Starbucks is normally seen as a coffee place, a work station place, a conversation place, a business meeting place, but as a "third space," it is a place where God is present and working in and through people. Your driveway is usually seen as a place to park your car, kids to play basketball, or to have a yard sale. But as a "third space" it is a place where God can be present in a conversation with a neighbor or family member. It takes practice and focus to see "third spaces."

Facilitator: pray for group as you begin this study.

Read Texts | 5 minutes |

Proclaiming the Kingdom
Matthew 26:6-13; Luke 7:36-50

6 Meanwhile, Jesus was in Bethany at the home of Simon, a man who had previously had leprosy. 7 While he was eating, a woman came in with a beautiful alabaster jar of expensive perfume and poured it over his head. 8 The disciples were indignant when they saw this. "What a waste!" they said. 9 "It could have been sold for a high price and the money given to the poor." 10 But Jesus, aware of this, replied, "Why criticize this woman for doing such a good thing to me? 11 You will always have the poor among you, but you will not always have me. 12 She has poured this perfume on me to prepare my body for burial. 13 I tell you the truth, wherever the Good News is preached throughout the world, this woman's deed will be remembered and discussed" (Matthew 26:6-13).

36 One of the Pharisees asked Jesus to have dinner with him, so Jesus went to his home and sat down to eat. 37 When a certain immoral woman from that city heard

he was eating there, she brought a beautiful alabaster jar filled with expensive perfume. [38] Then she knelt behind him at his feet, weeping. Her tears fell on his feet, and she wiped them off with her hair. Then she kept kissing his feet and putting perfume on them. [39] When the Pharisee who had invited him saw this, he said to himself, "If this man were a prophet, he would know what kind of woman is touching him. She's a sinner!"[40] Then Jesus answered his thoughts. "Simon," he said to the Pharisee, "I have something to say to you." "Go ahead, Teacher," Simon replied.[41] Then Jesus told him this story: "A man loaned money to two people—500 pieces of silver to one and 50 pieces to the other. [42] But neither of them could repay him, so he kindly forgave them both, canceling their debts. Who do you suppose loved him more after that?"[43] Simon answered, "I suppose the one for whom he canceled the larger debt." "That's right," Jesus said. [44] Then he turned to the woman and said to Simon, "Look at this woman kneeling here. When I entered your home, you didn't offer me water to wash the dust from my feet, but she has washed them with her tears and wiped them with her hair. [45] You didn't greet me with a kiss, but from the time I first came in, she has not stopped kissing my feet. [46] You neglected the courtesy of olive oil to anoint my head, but she has anointed my feet with rare perfume.[47] "I tell you, her sins—and they are many—have been forgiven, so she has shown me much love. But a person who is forgiven little shows only little love." [48] Then Jesus said to the woman, "Your sins are forgiven."[49] The men at the table said among themselves, "Who is this man, that he goes around forgiving sins?"[50] And Jesus said to the woman, "Your faith has saved you; go in peace" (Luke 7:36-50).

Group Work   25 minutes

Group(s) read and glean basic facts from texts in Matthew and Luke and record list on butcher paper, white board, or flipchart and in the journals.

As a regular practice doing this textual work all together with more than 6-8 participants is not practical given the limited time. However, for the first time your group(s) do this exercise of reading and gleaning the facts from the text, you may want to do this all together in order to set the example and expectations

Basic facts (not in participant's manual)

Matthew

- Jesus was in Bethany at the home of Simon (a leper)
- While eating, a woman came in and poured perfume from an expensive bottle on Jesus head
- Disciples were indignant seeing it as a waste—it could have been sold and the money given to the poor
- Jesus challenged them for criticizing the woman for doing such a good thing for Him
- Jesus said they would always have the poor but not always have Him
- Jesus said she had done this to prepare His body for burial
- Jesus said that wherever the Good News is preached in the world this woman's deed will be remembered and discussed

Luke

- Simon was a Pharisee
- A sinful woman brought an expensive bottle of perfume
- She knelt behind Jesus at his feet and wept
- Her tears fell on His feet and she wiped them with her hair and kept kissing His feet and putting perfume on them
- Simon was thinking if Jesus was a prophet He would know what kind of woman this was–a sinner
- Jesus answered his (Simon's) thoughts
  - Jesus told a story: Two debtors owed a man, one a small debt, and one a great debt. The man forgave both, canceling their debts
  - Jesus asked which one of the debtors would love the man more

- Simon said, "I suppose" the one with the larger debt
- Jesus said Simon was right and turned to the woman and said to Simon
  - Look at this woman
  - You did not offer me foot washing or a kiss or anointing
  - She has done all these things
- Jesus said her sins (many) are forgiven
- Jesus said forgiveness of much sin results in much love, forgiveness of little sin results in little love
- Jesus said to the woman your sins are forgiven
- The men at the table talked to each other saying who is this man that He forgives sin
- Jesus tells the woman, "Your faith has saved you. Go in peace."

Questions About the Facts

1. What is the significance of being invited to dinner at this person's house?

He is a well-known leader in the community and would attract a lot of attention and it would also give him prestige. He was a healed leper, once outcast himself. He should have known what the hospitality customs were and should have provided for them.

2. Why does the story talk about the woman's sin?

This is what the guests identified her as and also helps to demonstrate how deep the love of Christ is and why she was so demonstrative in her expression of love to Jesus.

3. What is the response of Simon and the others to the woman doing what she was doing?

They couldn't believe He was allowing her to touch him. They were judgmental and could not see her the way Jesus saw her. And they were totally unaware that they had failed to do what was customary and hospitable and that was exactly what this woman was doing. They could not see beyond their own personal experience to the bigger story being told.

4. Why did Jesus turn to the woman but talk to Simon?

He was keeping His attention on her as worthy of his attention and as an example for the others to follow. She was teaching Simon!

5. What is the significance of foot washing, kissing feet, anointing for the host/guest?

It was customary hospitality, but this woman was doing it above and beyond what was customary—matching the love of Jesus which was above and beyond anything she had ever experienced. But Jesus uses a common custom to also announce and reveal that He is being prepared for something much greater than the meal—His death and burial. She did not realize that she was being used to tell a much bigger story.

Compare and Contrast $\boxed{\text{10 minutes}}$

Use white board or butcher paper on tables or a flipchart. Write the following comparisons and contrasts.

Personal Story	Kingdom Story
A meal for insiders	A meal for outsiders
Simon's house where an uninvited woman enters	Third space created by Jesus for others to enter

Seen by disciples as sinner only	Seen by Jesus as one who needs grace and could serve Him
Excited about forgiveness (self)	Love and worship the Savior (kingdom)
Simple hospitality (feet, kiss, gift)	Preparation for cross (anointing for burial)
Sinful woman story	Jesus knows her story will be used to tell to others

Prayer — 5 minutes

The facilitator reads selected questions from below based on the responses from the group work. Leave a time of silence (20 seconds at least) in between each question you read for participants to pray silently.

In this way participants will be guided to pray silently through what they discovered about themselves and the living Christ from this story.

1. What is getting in the way of you seeing beyond your own personal salvation to see God's bigger story of kingdom work—what He is doing all around you?

2. How might your personal "space(s)" be a place for others to see God at work?

3. What parts of your own story could be told as part of God's BIG STORY?

4. Ask the Spirit of God to reveal to you, ways that you are self-focused instead of kingdom focused.

5. What customs/practices/habits are present in your life/environment that might actually be something God can use to help people to see Jesus more clearly?

6. Who might you see only as a sinner that Jesus may want you to see as a person that God loves and is at work in/can use to proclaim the greatness of his grace and Kingdom?

Review Session I assignments. | 5 minutes

Share Prayer

Clarify any questions, then end with Share Prayer.

In pairs tell each other your greatest fear/reservation regarding this experience. Then pray specifically for each other regarding this fear.

Session 1 Assignment

☐ **Pray** that the Lord will show you an opportunity to have a conversation with someone.

☐ **Have a conversation** with one person you do not know very well or at all or at least have never talked to about faith/God.

- If it does not come up naturally simply explain that you are trying to learn more about your personal faith and want to know what other people think and believe.

- Ask if they have ever had any experiences that they would describe as being spiritual and if they would tell you about one.

- Ask what they think it means to be a Christian.

- Ask what or who have they actually seen that reflects an expression of faith.

☐ **Observe** an environment (work, school, home, park, coffee shop) you are regularly in and think about how that space might be a "third space" for God to work.

☐ **Begin a Journal** and record (in word or pictures) your space observations. In your journal draw or find a picture showing your expectations/fears/reservations/hopes of this discipleship experience.

☐ **Review** Lectio divina. Information in Appendix I of Participant Manual.

☐ **Read** John 4:1-42, paying attention to parts of the story you might not have noticed before or that you have questions about and write or draw what stands out to you from this passage and be ready to share at the next *Groundings*

GROUNDINGS

Session 2

NOTICING GOD AT WORK

JOHN 4:1-42

Lectio Divina | 15 minutes |

Silence/Read/Listen/Reflect
Col. 1:15-20 (or other preselected text)

Reports | 15 minutes |

Leaders instruct participants to summarize 2 minutes each until
everyone has shared, then if there is more time some can expand.
(Encourage participants to use what they have recorded in their
journals.)

- At each table or in the whole group, share about what was learned from conversations/attempts at conversation.
- Share discovered third spaces. Each person simply names the "space" they were able to see differently and what helped them see it that way. (one min or less)

Large Group | 5 minutes |

Process for a few minutes with the whole group the learnings from these two assignments.

Make sure no one speaks long or more than once and that each table is heard from.

Prayer | 5 minutes |

At each table, pray for specific people and circumstances encountered from the interviews and pray for the spaces identified that the Spirit of God will help us open them up for God's Kingdom purposes.

Read Texts | 5 minutes |

Some Background Information for Leaders

The story of the woman at the well again is a story of both personal salvation (the woman) and the proclamation of the Kingdom of God. Reconciliation is also proclaimed—the breaking down of hostilities between disparate groups, i.e. men and women, Jew and Samaritan. We easily see and hear the story of the woman. It takes more focused attention to hear the BIG story of God's Kingdom being proclaimed. Below the text is a chart to compare both stories. Guide the group(s) by giving one example. Then have them compare and contrast what parts of the story are about the woman's personal salvation and what parts of the story are about the larger Kingdom story being proclaimed.

Noticing God at Work
John 4:1-42

[1] Jesus knew the Pharisees had heard that He was baptizing and making more disciples than John [2] (though Jesus himself didn't baptize them—His disciples did). [3] So he left Judea and returned to Galilee.

[4] He had to go through Samaria on the way. [5] Eventually He came to the Samaritan village of Sychar, near the field that Jacob gave to his son Joseph. [6] Jacob's well was there; and Jesus, tired from the long walk, sat wearily beside the well about noontime. [7] Soon a Samaritan woman came to draw water, and Jesus said to her, "Please give me a drink." [8] He was alone at the time because His disciples had gone into the village to buy some food.

[9] The woman was surprised, for Jews refuse to have anything to do with Samaritans. She said to Jesus, "You are a Jew, and I am a Samaritan woman. Why are you asking me for a drink?" [10] Jesus replied, "If you only knew the gift God has for you and who you are speaking to, you would ask me, and I would give you living water."

[11] "But sir, you don't have a rope or a bucket," she said, "and this well is very deep. Where would you get this living water? [12] And besides, do you think you're greater than our ancestor Jacob, who gave us this well? How can you offer better water than he and his sons and his animals enjoyed?"

[13] Jesus replied, "Anyone who drinks this water will soon become thirsty again. [14] But those who drink the water I give will never be thirsty again. It becomes a fresh, bubbling spring within them, giving them eternal life." [15] "Please, sir," the woman said, "give me this water! Then I'll never be thirsty again, and I won't have to come here to get water." [16] "Go and get your husband," Jesus told her. [17] "I don't have a husband," the woman replied.

Jesus said, "You're right! You don't have a husband— ¹⁸ for you have had five husbands, and you aren't even married to the man you're living with now. You certainly spoke the truth!"

¹⁹ "Sir," the woman said, "you must be a prophet. ²⁰ So tell me, why is it that you Jews insist that Jerusalem is the only place of worship, while we Samaritans claim it is here at Mount Gerizim, where our ancestors worshiped?"

²¹ Jesus replied, "Believe me, dear woman, the time is coming when it will no longer matter whether you worship the Father on this mountain or in Jerusalem. ²² You Samaritans know very little about the one you worship, while we Jews know all about Him, for salvation comes through the Jews. ²³ But the time is coming—indeed it's here now—when true worshipers will worship the Father in spirit and in truth. The Father is looking for those who will worship him that way. ²⁴ For God is Spirit, so those who worship him must worship in spirit and in truth."

²⁵ The woman said, "I know the Messiah is coming— the one who is called Christ. When He comes, He will explain everything to us." ²⁶ Then Jesus told her, "I am the Messiah!" ²⁷ Just then His disciples came back. They were shocked to find Him talking to a woman, but none of them had the nerve to ask, "What do you want with her?" or "Why are you talking to her?" ²⁸ The woman left her water jar beside the well and ran back to the village, telling everyone, ²⁹ "Come and see a man who told me everything I ever did! Could He possibly be the Messiah?" ³⁰ So the people came streaming from the village to see Him.

³¹ Meanwhile, the disciples were urging Jesus, "Rabbi, eat something."

³² But Jesus replied, "I have a kind of food you know nothing about." ³³ "Did someone bring Him food while we were gone?" the disciples asked each other.

³⁴ Then Jesus explained: "My nourishment comes from doing the will of God, who sent me, and from finishing His work. ³⁵ You know the saying, 'Four months between planting and harvest.' But I say, wake up and look around. The fields are already ripe for harvest. ³⁶ The harvesters are paid good wages, and the fruit they harvest is people brought to eternal life. What joy awaits both the planter and the harvester alike! ³⁷ You know the saying, 'One plants and another harvests.' And it's true. ³⁸ I sent you to harvest where you didn't plant; others had already done the work, and now you will get to gather the harvest."

³⁹ Many Samaritans from the village believed in Jesus because the woman had said, "He told me everything I ever did!" ⁴⁰ When they came out to see Him, they begged Him to stay in their village. So he stayed for two days, ⁴¹ long enough for many more to hear His message and believe. ⁴² Then they said to the woman, "Now we believe, not just because of what you told us, but because we have heard Him ourselves. Now we know that He is indeed the Savior of the world" (John 4:1-42).

In your journal, list the basic facts of the story. Pay attention to the differences between the woman and the disciples.

Basic Facts
- **Jesus had to go through Samaria and came to Sychar**
- **Field had been given to Joseph and Jacob's well was here**
- **Jesus was tired and weary and sat down by the well at noon**
- **A Samaritan woman came to draw water**
- **Jesus asked her for a drink**
- **He was alone because His disciples had gone to the village to buy food**
- **The woman was surprised because Jews refuse to have anything to do with Samaritans**

- The woman asked why Jesus asked her for water
- Jesus responded that if she only knew the gift God had for her and who He was that she would be the one asking and He would give her living water
- The woman observed that He had no rope or bucket and asked where He would get this water
- The woman understands Jesus was claiming to be greater than Jacob the giver of this well
- Jesus described the difference between this well water and the water He offers
- The woman wanted the water and thought this meant she would not have to come to the well again
- Jesus told her to call her husband and she replied she did not have a husband
- Jesus affirmed the truth and identified that she had five husbands and was living with a man now that she is not married to
- The woman said that Jesus must be a prophet
- The woman changed the subject and asked about the right place to worship
- Jesus announced that a time was coming when the place will not matter, that salvation has come through the Jews, and the Father wants worshipers who worship in spirit and truth
- The woman said she knew the Messiah would come who would explain everything
- Jesus told her He is that Messiah
- The disciples returned and were shocked to see Him talking to a woman (and were afraid to ask Him why He was talking to her and what about)
- The woman left her water jar and ran to the village telling everyone to come and see the man who told her everything about herself and wondered if He was the Messiah
- The people came streaming to see Him
- The disciples urged Jesus to eat and Jesus said He had food to eat they know nothing about

- The disciples were confused and thought He was talking about regular food
- Jesus explained His nourishment was doing God's will and finishing His work
- Jesus told them to pay attention and look around them (the woman and the people following her?) because the fields were ripe for harvest, the harvesters receive good wages and the fruit is people gaining eternal life
- Joy awaits those who plant and those who harvest
- Many Samaritans believed because of the woman and they begged Him to stay
- Jesus stayed, and many more believed that He was the Savior from hearing Him directly

Group Work

30 minutes

Questions About the Text

1. What is the significance of where Jesus encounters the woman?

Public space. Samaritan territory (not frequented by Jews). Well given by Jewish Father. Normal gathering place for daily chore early in the morning. Not normal for midday or woman to be alone. Place of resource for great need (water).

2. What does the text say about conversations between Jews and Samaritans and men and women?

Jews do not normally talk to Samaritans and men do not talk with women.

3. What does he engage in conversation with her about?

The burden and daily need of getting water.

4. What is the evidence of the earthly story?

The explanation of customs and taboos, the need for water and lunch.

5. What is the evidence of the Kingdom story?

Jesus knowing private things about the woman, the talk about "living water" and "never thirsting" or coming for "living water," reference to Jacob's well, talk about worship and what God requires.

6. How does Jesus connect them?

By starting with what she knows/has experienced and pointing to something bigger that she does not know/has not experienced.

7. Why do you think she asks about worship?

No right answer. The text does not say. But it likely has partly to do with the serious divide between Jew and Samaritan/male and female and that she was still trying to figure out why this Jewish man is talking to her at all. She seemed to perceive early on that there was something different/spiritual about Jesus so she may be testing Him or may really have always wondered about this question and thought He might know. Or she may have just been uncomfortable with the personal piercing questions/statements Jesus was making and tried to change the subject.

8. What is the significance of Jesus response?

He goes way beyond the scope of her question and cuts to the quick. Worship is about the heart and mind of the person, not the place, and one day the Kingdom will be in full view and these divisions will no longer exist or be relevant. And even though Jesus knows everything about her He has not excluded her from this future kingdom (like the Jewish religious leaders and the devout Jew would).

9. What is the woman's response to listening to Jesus? What is the evidence that she believes?

She excitedly leaves her water jar, runs, tells everyone, expresses He might be the Messiah, tells them to come and see for themselves.

10. What is the connection between Jesus conversation with the woman and His conversation with the disciples about food?

The disciples were more attentive to physical food than spiritual food and more attentive to daily tasks than Kingdom tasks.

11. Who in the story was doing Kingdom work?

Jesus and the Samaritan woman.

Compare and Contrast

There are other comparisons and contrasts, but these are the primary ones.

Experience of Woman	Experience of Disciples
Stops what she is doing to learn	Task oriented—get lunch (all of them?)
Almost immediately gets who He is	Still don't get who He is
So taken with Jesus she leaves task	So taken with task they leave Jesus
She tells/brings many to hear Him	They tell/bring no one to hear him
Her broken story becomes part of the big story	Their broken story becomes part of big story

Large Group   15 minutes

Work together to rewrite (out loud) the disciples' story so that they are Kingdom focused. Use the following questions to guide you in this exercise.

1. What would the disciples have done if they had seen Jesus as Messiah, the one who knew all about them—like the woman saw Him?

2. What would the disciples have done if they had seen the town where they got lunch as a "third space"?

3. What would the disciples have done if they had seen the well as a "third space?"
4. What would the disciples have done if they had seen God at work in the woman and her purpose in the kingdom?

Learning to Recognize and Tell Your Story   15 minutes

Do you have a "well story"—a time when you experienced the presence of Christ in an unusual way? Briefly summarize the place, time, and circumstances (2-3 minutes). If more than one table/group do this around tables. Write several bullet points of your story in your journal.

Review Session 2 Assignments	10 minutes

 Prayer

Pray in Pairs | 5 minutes |

- For the people that you will interview
- For each other's current story of life with Christ
- For this *Groundings Experience*

Session 2 Assignment

Another conversation: Discover someone else's story about their belief/unbelief in God

This conversation is not meant for you to argue, correct, explain, or defend anything. The primary objective is to learn to listen to others and notice God at work in their lives. You will do very little talking. Be curious. Ask questions. Try to understand their experience. [See *Groundings Stories*, "God in a Birdbath."]

❑   **What to ask:**
(These question prompts are guides *if* you need to get the conversation going. If the person opens up easily, simply listen and follow the conversation.)

Do you believe in God?

> If yes, what is the God that you believe in like, and where do these ideas come from?

> If not, why do you not believe?

> If yes, was there ever a "turning point" in your life when you sensed God's presence more in your daily life?

> If so, how and where?

> If not, what do you think other people are experiencing when they say they have experienced God in their lives? (no judgment).

I am keeping a journal about what I am learning. Do you mind if I take some notes as we talk?

Can you tell me more about that?

What did you mean when you said…...?

Have you ever experienced an extremely spiritual person?

Can you describe more about this person?

I want to learn from other people's experiences. Is there anything else you can tell me about your life story that might help me understand more about how you think God does work in everyday situations? Or why you think God doesn't?

Phrases you can say:
- Wow! That is very interesting.

- I really appreciate you being so honest.

- It sounds like you were/are really…

- I am amazed that…

- Hearing your story helps me understand mine more.

- Thank you for being willing to talk about this with me.

- Let me see if I heard you correctly. You said…

❑ **Your Personal Story/Timeline**

Identify and write or draw in your journal five key events in your life story—especially those events that, at the time or later in life, you realized these were times when God was working in you and through you. Using the intructions for Telling Your Story and the materials given to you by your *Groundings* Leader, begin making your Timeline.

❑ **Read**

Luke 10:25-37
As you read, pay attention to parts of the story you might not have noticed before or have questions about. Write or draw these in your journal, and come to the next class session prepared to share.

GROUNDINGS

Session 3

LISTENING TO OUR NEIGHBORS

LUKE 10:25-37

Lectio Divina | 15 minutes |

Respond
Colossians 1:15-20 (or other selected text)

Evaluation | 15 minutes |

What is happening outside and inside of you so far related to the *Groundings* experience? Your answers are not a report about your assignments; instead describe your feelings and experience.

Hopefully the students are familiar enough with each other to be comfortable to safely express the truth about what they are or are not doing and the range of emotions related to this discipleship experience. Make sure there is balanced reporting hearing both positive and negative experiences. And, help as many people as possible to share their experiences and feelings. These are not reports ABOUT their actual assignments. That comes next.

1. First—basic results—What have you done?

    ❑ I did not talk to anyone.
    ❑ I talked to my wife/husband.
    ❑ I forgot.
    ❑ I couldn't think of anyone to talk to.
    ❑ I talked to a neighbor.
    ❑ I talked to a stranger at Starbucks.
    ❑ I was afraid and just did not want to do it.

2. Second—feelings—What have you felt?

    ❑ Guilt – not doing the assignments
    ❑ Frustration – this class is not what I expected
    ❑ Anxious – don't know how to start conversations
    ❑ Excited – I am learning a lot from talking to others
    ❑ Embarrassed – I thought I knew more than I do
    ❑ Amazed – I am seeing God at work a lot more
    ❑ Confused – don't know what to think, mixed feelings

Reports | 20 minutes |

With your group, share your discoveries from your personal story/time line and your conversations.

> Each person will report what they learned from their conversations or interviews, not the details of the conversation/timeline. Every person should share briefly before anyone goes into more detail to ensure everyone has time to report.

Your time line/story

1. What did you realize about your own faith story that you had not realized before?

2. What and/or who stood out in your recollection?

3. Was anything missing from your stories?

Your interviews/conversations with others.

1. What surprised you?

2. What made you uncomfortable?

3. Did you ask questions? If so, what kind of questions did you ask?

4. How willing to talk were they? More or less than expected?

Large Group Share

Each group determines the top two discoveries from each experience of writing their story and interviewing another person. Then one person from each table/group shares these with the larger group.

> For example: "We all were surprised at how willing people were to talk" or "Everyone in our group was uncomfortable beginning the conversation."

Prayer

Pray in Pairs | 5 minutes |

- For those struggling with the assignments.

Share in Pairs

- Who is a person that helped you to see God at work, and how did they help you?
- Pray, giving thanks for these people.

Read Text | 5 minutes |

Listening to My Neighbors
Luke 10:25-37

25 One day an expert in religious law stood up to test Jesus by asking Him this question: "Teacher, what should I do to inherit eternal life?" 26 Jesus replied, "What does the law of Moses say? How do you read it?" 27 The man answered, "You must love the Lord your God with all your heart, all your soul, all your strength, and all your mind.' And, 'Love your neighbor as yourself.'" 28 "Right!" Jesus told him. "Do this and you will live!" 29 The man wanted to justify his actions, so he asked Jesus, "And who is my neighbor?"

30 Jesus replied with a story: "A Jewish man was traveling from Jerusalem down to Jericho, and he was attacked by bandits. They stripped him of his clothes, beat him up, and left him half dead beside the road. 31 "By chance a priest came along. But when he saw the man lying there, he crossed to the other side of the road and passed him by. 32 A Temple assistant walked over and looked at him lying there, but he also passed by on the other side. 33 "Then a despised Samaritan

came along, and when he saw the man, he felt compassion for him. [34] Going over to him, the Samaritan soothed his wounds with olive oil and wine and bandaged them. Then he put the man on his own donkey and took him to an inn, where he took care of him. [35] The next day he handed the innkeeper two silver coins, telling him, 'Take care of this man. If his bill runs higher than this, I'll pay you the next time I'm here.' [36] "Now which of these three would you say was a neighbor to the man who was attacked by bandits?" Jesus asked. [37] The man replied, "The one who showed him mercy." Then Jesus said, "Yes, now go and do the same" (Luke 10:25-37).

Basic Facts

- An expert in the law stood up to test Jesus
- He asked what he needed to do to inherit eternal life
- Jesus responded with two questions—What does the law say? How do you read it?
- The expert responded—love God and your neighbor
- Jesus responded that he was right and tells him to do it and he will live
- The expert wanted to justify his actions so asks who is his neighbor
- Jesus replied with a story:
    - A Jewish man was traveling from Jerusalem to Jericho
    - The man was attacked by bandits who strip him, beat him, and leave him for dead
    - By chance a priest came along and saw him and went to the other side of the road and kept going
    - A temple assistant (Levite) walked by and looked at him but also went to the other side of the road and kept walking

- A despised Samaritan came along, saw him, and had compassion.
  - Soothed his wounds and bandaged them
  - Put the man on his donkey, took him to an inn and took care of him overnight
  - The next day gave the innkeeper money (two days' wages) and told him:
    - To take care of the man
    - And if any additional cost of care, he would pay when he returned
- Jesus then asked a question: Which of these three would you say was a neighbor to the man who was attacked?
- The expert replied: The one who showed him mercy
- Jesus replied: Now go and do the same

Group Work   40 minutes

Questions About the Text

As a group, discuss the text. Record facts and questions in your journal.

Questions About the Facts

1. What made the man an expert in the law?

Vs. 25 He was an educated lawyer or a scribe whose job it was to know the law and interpret it for the uneducated.

2. Was the man primarily interested in the answer to his question? What about the text indicates otherwise?

Vs. 25 He was testing Jesus.

3. Is it important that Jesus asks two questions in response rather than one? What is the difference between the two questions?

Vs. 26 Jesus tested him! He knew what the law said and Jesus had him say it out loud but then asked the more important question of what he thought it meant—how did HE READ it?

4. Was the expert quoting from the law? Yes. If so where?

Vs. 27 Deuteronomy 6:5 and Leviticus 19:18

5. What actions was the expert trying to justify?

Vs 29 The Jews believed that only fellow Jews were their neighbors and that the law excluded all others.

6. Why do you think Jesus describes the second man as a temple assistant?

Probably a Levite who served the priests in the temple. Jesus included all who served the Lord in the temple in this lesson. Also demonstrating that the attitudes and actions of the priests were reflected in others around them.

7. Who despised the Samaritan man?

Jews despised the Samaritans because they were Jews who had intermarried with Gentiles and who did not practice Judaism according to the letter of the law. They were "half breeds" and unclean by their association with Gentiles and outcasts in the eyes of the educated religious leaders.

8. What was the extent of the Samaritans care? Why was this important?

Above and beyond the call of duty. More than helpful, excessively generous. Because it demonstrates the radically different kind of love that the law requires of all people for all people and ultimately reflects the kind of love God has shown us.

9. What is indicated about the Samaritan man by the fact that he could leave this sick man at the inn saying he would return and pay any extra cost later?

This man had a reputation of integrity and honesty. He was known for his word and his way of living and trusted by others. He may have also left a sizable amount with the inn keeper indicating his ability to pay and his reciprocal trust of the inn keeper.

10. Why is it important that Jesus asks a question after telling the story?

He again tested the expert law keeper on his understanding of what the law MEANT rather than what the law said. And He forced him to say out loud what was obvious. In doing so the expert in the law reveals his own breaking of the law of neighborliness in his attitude toward the Gentiles/Samaritans.

11. Is Jesus answer a direct answer to the expert's original question or something else?

Yes, but Jesus went further. The expert in the law believed that keeping the law, as he understood it, was the way to eternal life. Jesus revealed that it is not only outward behavior but inward attitudes and beliefs (heart) that determined whether or not a person is keeping the law. In doing so Jesus demonstrated that it is impossible to earn eternal life by doing everything right—what He will teach later explicitly when He says "you have heard that it was said, but I say." (Matthew 5)

Questions for Table Discussion   5 minutes

1. Do we ever use "questions" for a reason other than finding an answer?

2. How do we respond to challenges to our faith or convictions?

3. How did the Pharisee's "questions" affect his neighborliness?

4. What are obstacles to *our* neighborliness?

5. Pray for each other to see and respond to your neighbors.

Identify Your Neighbor   5 minutes

1. Discuss how you can discern *who* is your neighbor?

2. Talk about who God might be leading you to in order to be a neighbor like the one in the story of the Good Samaritan?

3. How are we all like the man in the ditch?

4. Each person identifies at least one person.

5. Table group help brainstorm how each of these persons might be approached.

Review Session 3 Assignments   5 minutes

 Prayer   5 minutes

In pairs, pray for each other and the person each of you has identified.

Session 3 Assignment

❑ **Plan a Neighborhood Observation Exercise**

Go out together (in pairs or together to a larger space)
For Questions to ask and things to look for, see **Neighborhood Observation Exercise** in Appendix III. You can make this an assignment in between session 3 and 4, or you can do it as part of session 4.

❑ **Identify two places in your space where you encounter "neighbors."**

Take photos of these places to share with the group.

❑ **Try to encounter at least one such neighbor and record the experience.**

In your journal, write or draw about the experience.

❑ **Continue working on your story timeline.**

❑ **Read** Luke 19:1-10

GROUNDINGS

Session 4

GIVING AND RECEIVING HOSPITALITY

LUKE 19:1-10

Lectio Divina | 15 minutes |

Contemplate
Colossians 1:15-20 (or other selected text)

Going-Out-to-Observe Reports | 30 minutes |

Use neighborhood observation questions found in Appendix III. Go out in twos and threes. Each pair or triplet walking in a different direction from where you are meeting. Total time should be about 30 minutes.

From neighborhood discoveries

1. What did you see and hear in your "neighborhood?" Or the neighborhood you walked?

2. Did you observe or can you imagine any "third spaces" there?

3. What obstacles (mental or physical) did you encounter?

4. What is the most difficult place you entered? Who were the most challenging people to see or approach like the neighborhood/neighbor that Jesus describes?

One neighbor encounter

1. What conversations did you overhear?

2. What conversations did you join? How?

3. Were you able to hear or see God at work in this conversation?

Read Text | 5 minutes |

Some Background Information for Leaders

The story of the Zacchaeus turns everything upside down. Again it is a personal story and a kingdom story. Once again Jesus is using an individual story to proclaim the bigger Kingdom story. This time it is all about who is hosting who. And when we answer this question all spaces change. All spaces become a space where Jesus can host us and others and use our spaces and our lives to proclaim the Good News of the Kingdom. The disciples in this story are more silent.

Giving and Receiving Hospitality
Luke 19:1-10

[1] Jesus entered Jericho and made his way through the town. [2] There was a man there named Zacchaeus. He was the chief tax collector in the region, and he had become very rich. [3] He tried to get a look at Jesus, but he was too short to see over the crowd. [4] So he ran ahead and climbed a sycamore-fig tree beside the road, for Jesus was going to pass that way. [5] When Jesus came by, He looked up at Zacchaeus and called him by name. "Zacchaeus!" He said. "Quick, come down! I must be a guest in your home today." [6] Zacchaeus quickly climbed down and took Jesus to his house in great excitement and joy. [7] But the people were displeased. "He has gone to be the guest of a notorious sinner," they grumbled. [8] Meanwhile, Zacchaeus stood before the Lord and said, "I will give half my wealth to the poor, Lord, and if I have cheated people on their taxes, I will give them back four times as much!" [9] Jesus responded, "Salvation has come to this home today, for this man has shown himself to be a true son of Abraham. [10] For the Son of Man came to seek and save those who are lost" (Luke 19:1-10).

Basic Facts

- Jesus was passing through Jericho
- A man named Zacchaeus was there—a rich tax collector
- Zacchaeus wanted to see who Jesus was but the crowd and his height prevented him
- Zacchaeus ran ahead and climbed a tree (to try to see Jesus)
- Jesus came to the place (where Zacchaeus was) and looked up and said to him:
    - Zacchaeus, hurry down for I must stay at your house today
- Zacchaeus hurried down and was happy to welcome Jesus (to his house)

- Everyone who saw this began to grumble. They said, He has gone to be a guest of a sinner
- Zacchaeus said to Jesus
  - Look, half of my possessions I will give to the poor
  - And, if I have cheated anyone anything, I will give back four times as much
- Jesus said to Zacchaeus and those listening
  - Today salvation has come to this house
  - He (Zacchaeus) too is a son of Abraham
  - The Son of Man came to seek and save the lost

Group Work | 30 minutes |

Questions About the Text

Identify the basic facts and record them and any questions you have about the story.

Questions about the Facts

1. What is the significance of Jesus passing through and then going to Zacchaeus' house?

He was very attentive to His surroundings and the people He was encountering. And He was attentive to people's response to Him. He changed His plans to do this.

2. How did people feel about tax collectors?

Loathed them, hated them, despised them. They got rich off cheating people and were "collaborators" with the enemy, the occupying Romans.

3. What is implied by the fact that he was a rich tax collector? Is this informed at all by Zacchaeus' promise in vs. 8? By how the grumblers categorize Zacchaeus?

Zacchaeus reveals that he has defrauded others, another word for cheating and being dishonest with them in regard to taxes. They call him a sinner but the text does not say why, but does imply whatever he did that made him a sinner was very public.

4. How do you think Zacchaeus felt when Jesus asked to come to his house?

Amazed, shocked, excited, afraid.

5. How did the other people feel about this?

Shocked, confused, frustrated, angry, jealous.

6. Who is the "host" in this story?

Jesus does the inviting and creates the space by His presence.

7. What are the "third spaces" in this story?

The village street, the tree where Jesus stops, Zacchaeus' house.

8. Why do you think Jesus said that salvation had come to this house?

Zacchaeus showed a desire to follow Jesus by a change of heart and behavior, exactly what Jesus was looking for.

9. What is the significance of Jesus calling Zacchaeus a "son of Abraham"?

Jesus is teaching that being related to God, being one of God's children is not simply about genetics, or physical birth heritage. It is about having a heart open to what God wants and open to following where God leads. THIS makes a person a child of Abraham, a child of God.

10. How does Jesus feel about sinners? What does He do about sinners? (vs. 10)

> He takes the initiative to find them and to save them from their lost, sinful ways. He refers to them as part of the family (sons of Abraham) and says that He came to seek them and save them.

Definition of hospitality based on Luke 19: *Welcoming* **and** *being with and accepting another (others)*

1. What makes people feel welcome?

2. What makes people feel unwelcome?

3. How can we "be with others" in space that is foreign/not ours?

4. How can we communicate acceptance in a foreign space?

5. What are ways to make "third space" places hospitable?

Questions for Table Discussion | 5 minutes |

Discerning

1. What are the obstacles you have to being hospitable?

2. What are the obstacles you have to accepting hospitality?

3. Who are the people you could invite into your space or a third space?

4. Who are the people that you might need to accept hospitality from?

Review Assignments for Session 4 **5 minutes**

 Prayer   10 minutes

The leader will designate someone to start at the table(s) and that person will pray for the person to their right:

- That obstacles will be removed
- That space (theirs or third spaces) will open up
- That they will see at least one person to invite
- That they will be open to at least one invitation of others

Session 4 Assignment

❑ **Invite someone(s) into your space and record the experiment in your journal.**

How did you identify the person(s)?

How did it feel to invite them?

How did they respond?

What was the best part and worst part of the experience?

❑ **Accept an invitation into someone else's space and record the experience in your journal.**

How did you recognize the invitation?

How did it feel to accept it?

How did you respond

What was the best and worst part of the whole experience?

❑ **Finish your story or time line. Come to the next gathering prepared to share parts of your story with your small group.**

❑ **Read John 3:1-10, 14-17. Record new insights and questions in your journal.**

GROUNDINGS

Session 5

UNDERSTANDING THE MISSION OF GOD

JOHN 3:1-10, 14-17

Evaluation | 20 minutes |

Overall feedback.

1. What progress have you personally made from these *Groundings Experiences:*

... In approaching the Scripture more open minded/hearted?

... In listening?

... In noticing God at work in and around you?

... In seeing and using "third spaces?

... In telling your own story?

2. What do you want to experience/do yet before you complete this experience?

Lectio Divina 20 minutes

Resolve
Colossians 1:15-20 (or other text)

Reports 20 minutes

At your table, share about your experience giving and receiving hospitality. Share at least one "aha" moment with the large group.

In your group, pray for people and circumstances described in reports.

Read Text 5 minutes

Some Background Information for Leaders

The story of the Nicodemus again highlights that having information about God is not knowing God, and that sometimes knowing a lot can get in the way. There is no individual contrast to Nicodemus in this story. The contrast is every person because Jesus wants the

Good News to be proclaimed to all creatures. Once again Jesus uses the question of an inquirer, perhaps not trying to justify himself this time, but certainly needing to see the bigger kingdom Jesus has come to establish. Once again, a learned Jew is missing the BIG story of God's Kingdom being proclaimed. Guide the group in exploring our personal obstacles (compare and contrast: some are the same, some are different) to understanding Jesus Kingdom story.

Understanding the Mission of God
John 3:1-10, 14-17

[1] There was a man named Nicodemus, a Jewish religious leader who was a Pharisee. [2] After dark one evening, he came to speak with Jesus. "Rabbi," he said, "we all know that God has sent you to teach us. Your miraculous signs are evidence that God is with you." [3] Jesus replied, "I tell you the truth, unless you are born again, you cannot see the Kingdom of God." [4] "What do you mean?" exclaimed Nicodemus. "How can an old man go back into his mother's womb and be born again?" [5] Jesus replied, "I assure you, no one can enter the Kingdom of God without being born of water and the Spirit. [6] Humans can reproduce only human life, but the Holy Spirit gives birth to spiritual life. [7] So don't be surprised when I say, 'You must be born again.' [8] The wind blows wherever it wants. Just as you can hear the wind but can't tell where it comes from or where it is going, so you can't explain how people are born of the Spirit." [9] "How are these things possible?" Nicodemus asked. [10] Jesus replied, "You are a respected Jewish teacher, and yet you don't understand these things?

[14] And as Moses lifted up the bronze snake on a pole in the wilderness, so the Son of Man must be lifted up, [15] so that everyone who believes in him will have eternal life. [16] "For this is how God loved the world: He gave his one and only Son, so that everyone who believes in him will not perish but have eternal life. [17] God sent his Son into the world not to judge the world, but to save the world through him (John 3:1-10; 14-17).

Group Work | 40 minutes |

Questions About the Text

Identify the basic facts and record them and any questions you have about the story.

Questions about the Facts

Basic

- There was a leader of the Jews, a Pharisee named Nicodemus
- He came to see Jesus at night
- He called Jesus Rabbi and said
    - We know that You are a teacher come from God.
    - No one can do the signs You do apart from the presence of God
- Jesus said to him
    - Truly I tell you, no one can see the Kingdom of God without being born again
- Nicodemus said
    - How can anyone be born after they have grown old?
    - Can they enter their mother's womb and be born?
- Jesus said,
    - Truly, no one can enter the Kingdom of God without being born of water and Spirit
    - What is born of flesh is flesh
    - What is born of Spirit is spirit
    - Don't be surprised that I said you must be born from above
    - The wind blows where it chooses and you hear the sound but you do not know where it comes from or where it goes
    - So it is with everyone who is born of the Spirit

- **Nicodemus said**
  - **How can these things be?**
- **Jesus said,**
    - **Are you a teacher of Israel yet you do not understand these things?**
    - **For God so loved the world that He gave His only Son**
    - **Everyone who believes in Him will not perish but have eternal life**
    - **God did not send His son to condemn but to save the world**

1. Why do you think Nicodemus came at night?

It does not say, but the fact that it is stated so explicitly makes it important, especially since Jesus was so available in public during the day. And, given other passages in John about Nicodemus (7:50; 19:39) Nicodemus was part of the powerful and antagonistic Pharisees. He was being drawn to Jesus and his message but at this point was still very cautious and unsure. He was likely afraid of being seen with Jesus and afraid of losing his position and status.

2. What did Nicodemus know about Jesus?

That He was a teacher, come from God, and had been doing signs/miracles that were interpreted by some as evidence of the presence of God.

3. What did he not know? (What did Jesus have to tell him?)

What it meant to be born from above, and the reality of spiritual birth that does not happen automatically because you are physically born (as a Jew even!) and that God sent Him (Jesus) out of love for the whole world, and whoever believes in Jesus will be saved.

4. How does Jesus address Nicodemus?

Not by name, but appeals to his desire to know the truth. "Verily, verily," or "I tell you the truth" was a common statement indicating absolute fact.

5. What does Jesus know about him?

That he is a teacher of the law and yet does not know spiritual things that the law points to. He knows outward signs of God's presence, but has not experienced the inward sign—the Spirit of God living in him.

6. What is the evidence that Nicodemus is thinking in earthly/physical terms?

He is talking and thinking about the letter of the law and physical birth, the size of a woman's womb and being born of a woman.

7. What is the evidence that Jesus is speaking in physical and spiritual terms?

He acknowledges what Nicodemus has said and says there is more. Water and Spirit are necessary for spiritual birth and human beings cannot "see" the Spirit but they can see the evidence of it, just like the wind.

8. How is being born of the Spirit like the wind?

We cannot see the Spirit that causes us to be born again, but we can see the evidence of it—what it does in our lives and the way we live.

9. What does Jesus communicate about salvation (being born again) by using this analogy?

It is not a result of knowledge of the law or right actions. It is something only the Spirit of God can do. But Jesus implies that seeking it, as Nicodemus might be doing, is important in order for the Spirit to give new life.

10. How is Nicodemus' story being used by Jesus?

His disciples probably were with Him and hearing this as well. (3:22) Once again, Jesus takes a simple statement— "I know You are a teacher come from God by the miracles that You do"—and turns it into a lesson on who He really is and what He has come to do. He reveals His mission is greater than the miracles that Nicodemus has seen. The REAL miracle is a person being born again of the Spirit and brought from death (perishing) to life (eternal).

Compare and Contrast

Group uses journal or butcher paper on tables then collate on white board or butcher paper on wall. Participants record biggest take-aways in their journals.

Compare and contrast the obstacles to understanding spiritual things then and now. Some are the same, some are different. List as many as you can think of.

Then:	Now:
Mosaic Law	Christian culture/Church experience/Rules
Fear of reputation	What people think (who are these people today?)
Political and faith structures	Time/Attention to immediate visible world

What can be seen	Not knowing what to look for
No learning/Have answers	Uncertainty/Suspicion/Pluralism
Self-righteousness	Individualism

Prayer | 5 minutes |

Each table break up in pairs and pray for each other about the obstacles each is experiencing in understanding and living out spiritual things.

Using the text and the obstacles discovered guide them in listening for a word or phrase about understanding the mission of God. Then have them pray in partners regarding specific obstacles in their lives.

The leader will designate someone to start at the table(s) and that person will pray for the person to their right.

Group Sharing | 15 minutes |

This is a participant directed time. Encourage them that it is completely open. There is no agenda.

What do you want to or need to express or talk about or ask related to your *Groundings Experience*?

Review Session 5 Assignments | 5 minutes |

Session 5 Assignment

❑ **Fasting.**

Each person commits to fasting that is appropriate for them. It can be one meal or one day or one particular food/drink item for an extended period of time or it can be an activity like watching TV or texting. Journal about this experience. Write about how you decided, and what you decided and why. Write about how it felt or impacted your everyday experience. (See Fasting in the Appendix IV.)

❑ **Interview or have a discussion with an unchurched person**.

Ask what they think God is (or is not) doing in the world.

Listen for obstacles that keep them from seeing God.

Listen for clues that help them see.

❑ **Where do you most clearly see God at work in your life right now?**

❑ **Identify (draw or write in your journal) something in your life that needs transformation as a result of understanding God's mission and your part in it.**

What in your life needs to be reoriented?
What priorities need to be rearranged?

❑ **Begin to think about how you might take this *Groundings Experience* and pass it on.**

Come prepared to talk about it at our final gathering.

a.   Is there a particular person (or two) you have a relationship with that you could approach about doing this with you?

b.   Is there a group you are part of that might be willing to have you lead them through this experience?

c.   What would you need to feel confident in helping someone else or a group go through Groundings?

❑   **Plan and delegate the work for a shared meal for the last session**

GROUNDINGS

Session 6

GROUNDINGS: WHAT'S NEXT?

A MINI RETREAT

SHARE A MEAL TOGETHER | 60 minutes |

Lectio Divina | 20 minutes |

From Read to Resolve
Colossians 1:15-20 (or other selected text)

Reflection on all Five Texts | 20 minutes |

My favorite text is…

A common theme in all of the texts was …

Something I never saw before was …

I realized more than ever that Jesus ...

My other Bible reading has been ...

Small Group $\boxed{\text{20 minutes}}$

1. Share the biggest take-away from various narratives.

2. How have you grown in listening to God/noticing him at work?

3. How has it affected your discipleship?

4. How are you following Jesus:
    ... In your faith community?

    ... As you go out from this experience?

    ... In your other main contexts/places?

5. Share the highlights of stories of engagement with others?

6. What was most difficult for you? What was easy for you?

7. What do you need going forward in order to:
    ... continue to be a follower of Christ?

    ... be open to hearing a fresh word from the Scripture?

    ... notice God at work in and around you and in others?

    ... be available to do Kingdom work in Christ's name?

    ... continue to be transformed by the mission of God?

8. What did you learn from your fasting experience?

9. How will this experience affect you from now on?

Large Group | 20 minutes |

Large group sharing summary of learnings if there are more than one table group.

Guided Prayer from the Texts | 30 minutes |

Pray to become bold and enthusiastic proclaimers of the Kingdom Jesus is building. *(The woman who anointed Jesus at Simon's house)*

Pray to be more aware and notice God at work in unlikely people we encounter. *(The woman at the well)*

Pray for your "neighborhood" and other third spaces that can be a "neighborhood" for the love of Jesus to be proclaimed. *(The Good Samaritan)*

Pray to be a courageous giver and receiver of hospitality. *(Zacchaeus)*

Pray to increasingly know what it means to understand and live out the mission of God as your primary way of life, a reflection of the image of Jesus to the world. *(Nicodemus)*

Groundings Next | 20 minutes |

First share together in small groups with a member of each group recording the answers to the questions below. Then summarize these answers in the large group.

1. What will the next step be for your continued discipleship grounding? Practices? What part of *Groundings* will you continue? What will you not continue?

2. What are the possible venues in your sphere of influence to pass on this experience?

3. What way is God leading you to pass this experience on? Who? Where?

4. Would you be comfortable facilitating this experience by yourself? With another person?

5. What do you need to be confident in facilitating another person or group?

Review Assignments for Session 6. | **10 minutes** |

Prayer | 10 minutes |

Facilitators pray for the participants and for the continued work of God in their everyday lives and for others who will go through this experience by their leadership.

- For each other going forward
- For the *Groundings Experience* to transform more disciples of Christ

Session 6 Assignment

Final Assignment to complete in the next 30 days:

❏ In the next week share with at least two different people in a regular conversation what you learned in *Groundings*.

❏ In the next 30 days, continue to pray and determine where/how you will pass on the *Groundings Experience* and let your *Groundings* leader know.

❏ Continue being grounded in Christ, paying attention to what God is doing in and through and around you every day.

❏ Continue to read and listen to the Scripture with an open heart and mind with the expectation that you *will* encounter the living and powerful Christ through the Word.

Appendix I

Lectio Divina

"Somehow, I had fallen into a pattern of using the Scriptures as a tool to accomplish utilitarian purposes rather experiencing them primarily as a place of intimacy with God for my own soul's sake."
~Ruth Haley Barton

Groundings and Lectio Divina

There are a variety of configurations for *lectio divina*. For the purpose of our *Groundings Experience* we will be using the following:

Silence – every experience will begin with some time to clear out all the mental clutter and calm the emotional landscape and relax whatever physical demands are present.

Read/Listen – being open to hearing fresh from whatever Scripture is being read out loud. Two or three difference voices will be used to help you do this.

Reflect – to spend time thinking about how whatever stood out to you/spoke to you is connected to your everyday life experience right now.

Respond – this step is not a "what do I do?" but a very open and honest attention to how you are feeling and what you are thinking about what you have heard and reflected on.

Contemplate (Rest) – returning to what you heard and resting in it as from the love of God.

Resolve - this is often where we go to right away when we are approaching a text analytically! But this comes most clearly only after we have spent the time doing the other parts of *lectio divina*. Sometimes the "resolve" develops more as you continue to "hear" and "reflect" and "respond" to this word throughout the coming days.

Some participants may have learned the discipline of lectio divina. For most it will be new. And some may struggle with the practice. The value of lectio is in being open and willing to listen to God in this way.

Encourage everyone to continue to submit and trust God with the results. Session one of *Groundings* will give the overview of lectio divina and then the first session/experience will teach only Silence and Read/Listen. Then each subsequent session/experience will add one more step in lectio divina as outlined above.

We introduce this discipline slowly intentionally. Be gracious with those who struggle with lectio. The final session/experience will include the full lectio divina discipline.

Appendix II

Lectio Divina Texts

Colossians 1:15-20

Christ is the visible image of the invisible God.
He existed before anything was created and is supreme over all creation, for through him God created everything in the heavenly realms and on earth.

He made the things we can see and the things we can't see—such as thrones, kingdoms, rulers, and authorities in the unseen world.

Everything was created through him and for him.
He existed before anything else, and he holds all creation together.

Christ is also the head of the church, which is his body. He is the beginning, supreme over all who rise from the dead.

So he is first in everything.

For God in all his fullness was pleased to live in Christ, and through him God reconciled everything to himself. He made peace with everything in heaven and on earth by means of Christ's blood on the cross.

Matthew 16:24-26

Then Jesus told his disciples, "If any want to become my followers, let them deny themselves and take up their cross and follow me.

For those who want to save their life will lose it, and those who lose their life for my sake will find it.

For what will it profit them if they gain the whole world but forfeit their life? Or what will they give in return for their life?"

Psalm 23:1-6

The Lord is my shepherd; I shall not want.
He makes me to lie down in green pastures: he leads me beside still waters; he leads me in the right paths for his name's sake.

Even though I walk through the darkest valley, I fear no evil; for you are with me; your rod and your staff—they comfort me.

You prepare a table before me in the presence of my enemies; you anoint my head with oil; my cup overflows.

Surely goodness and mercy shall follow me all the days of my life, and I shall dwell in the house of the Lord my whole life long.

Philippians 4:8

Finally, beloved, whatever is true, whatever is honorable, whatever is just,whatever is pure, whatever is pleasing, whatever is commendable, if there is any excellence and if there is anything worthy of praise, think about these things.

Keep on doing the things that you have learned and received and heard and seen in me,and the God of peace will be with you.

Appendix III

Neighborhood Observation Exercise

Wondering and noticing as you go?

- As you begin, take a quick survey. What do you see that is different in each direction from where you stand?

- As you walk, what do you notice about the entrances to the houses/buildings/stores?

- What does the signage reveal?

- What "feel" does this neighborhood have?

- What are the signs of stability? Transience?

- Is there any open space? Is it being used? How?

- Are there any churches or religious/spiritually focused buildings or businesses? What do they communicate?

- What is the time of day? How many people are out and about? Who are they? Age, gender, ethnicity, etc.? What are they doing? Is there interaction between them?

- Does the area seem to invite people to come out or not? Why?

- Which of these spaces invites *you*? Does not invite *you*? Why or why not?

When you've completed your walk:

- What stood out most about the place you went? Good? Bad?

- What was something you noticed that you had never noticed before?

- Did you see or hear anything that seemed evidence of God's presence?

- Did you see any space that you can imagine could be a place or way for us at SCPC to enter into in order to participate in what God might be doing in that place or could do in that place if we were to offer ourselves?

- Any other observations/feelings/conclusions as a result of your exploring this neighborhood?

Appendix IV

Fasting

Old Testament

Psalm 35:13; 69:10; 109:24—fasting as an **outcry** to God in relation to facing oppressive enemies

New Testament
Matthew 4:1-11

> Then Jesus was led up by the Spirit into the wilderness to be tempted by the devil. He fasted forty days and forty nights, and afterwards he was famished. The tempter came and said to him, "If you are the Son of God, command these stones to become loaves of bread." But he answered, "It is written, 'One does not live by bread alone, but by every word that comes from the mouth of God.'" Then the devil took him to the holy city and placed him on the pinnacle of the temple, saying to him, "If you are the Son of God, throw yourself down; for it is written, 'He will command his angels concerning you,' and 'On their hands they will bear you up, so that you will not dash your foot against a stone.'" Jesus said to him, "Again it is written, 'Do not put the Lord your God to the test.'" Again, the devil took him to a very high mountain and showed him all the kingdoms of the world and their splendor; and he said to him, "All these I will give you, if you will fall down and worship me." Jesus said to him, "Away with you, Satan! for it is written, 'Worship the Lord your God, and serve only him.'" Then the devil left him, and suddenly angels came and waited on him.

Matthew 6:16-18

> "And whenever you fast, do not look dismal, like the hypocrites, for they disfigure their faces so as to show others that they are fasting. Truly I tell you, they have

received their reward. But when you fast, put oil on your head and wash your face, so that your fasting may be seen not by others but by your Father who is in secret; and your Father who sees in secret will reward you.

Matthew 9:14–18

"Why do we and the Pharisees fast often, but your disciples do not fast?" And Jesus said to them, "The wedding guests cannot mourn as long as the bridegroom is with them, can they? The days will come when the bridegroom is taken away from them, and then they will fast. No one sews a piece of unshrunk cloth on an old cloak, for the patch pulls away from the cloak, and a worse tear is made. Neither is new wine put into old wineskins; otherwise, the skins burst, and the wine is spilled, and the skins are destroyed; but new wine is put into fresh wineskins, and so both are preserved."

Luke 2:36–38

There was also a prophet, Anna the daughter of Phanuel, of the tribe of Asher. She was of a great age, having lived with her husband seven years after her marriage, then as a widow to the age of eighty-four. She never left the temple but worshiped there with fasting and prayer night and day. At that moment she came, and began to praise God and to speak about the child to all who were looking for the redemption of Jerusalem.

Luke 18:9–14

He also told this parable to some who trusted in themselves that they were righteous and regarded others with contempt: "Two men went up to the temple to pray, one a Pharisee and the other a tax collector. The Pharisee, standing by himself, was praying thus, 'God, I thank you that I am not like other people: thieves, rogues, adulterers, or even like this tax collector. I fast twice a week; I give a tenth of all my income.' But the tax collector, standing far off, would not even look up to heaven, but was beating his breast and saying, 'God, be merciful to me, a sinner!' I tell you, this man went down to his home justified rather than the other; for all who exalt themselves will be humbled, but all who humble themselves will be exalted."

Acts 13:1–3

Now in the church at Antioch there were prophets and teachers: Barnabas, Simeon who was called Niger, Lucius of Cyrene, Manaen a member of the court of Herod the ruler, and Saul. While they were worshiping the Lord and fasting, the Holy Spirit said, "Set apart for me Barnabas and Saul for the work to which I have called them." Then after fasting and praying they laid their hands on them and sent them off.

Acts 14:21–23

After they had proclaimed the good news to that city and had made many disciples, they returned to Lystra, then on to Iconium and Antioch. There they strengthened the souls of the disciples and encouraged them to continue in the faith, saying, "It is through many persecutions that we must enter the kingdom of God." And after they had appointed elders for them in each church, with prayer and fasting they entrusted them to the Lord in whom they had come to believe.

From the *Dictionary of Jesus and the Gospels*

Fasting in the Gospels

Jesus and His Disciples' Fasting.

When queried about his disciples' practice, Jesus first quotes what is likely a proverbial saying about the inappropriateness of wedding guests fasting while the bridegroom (*see* Bride, Bridegroom) is in their company (cf. *Gos. Thom.* 104) or the wedding festival is in progress. Taking up a common symbol for the age of salvation, a wedding celebration, and identifying himself with the bride groom, though probably not messianically, he explains that fasting will only come into consideration when he is removed from them (Mk 2:19–20).

. . . And he does not prescribe fasting in the future so much as contrast the present fellowship and joy of the age of salvation being initiated with the future sadness associated with his forceful removal from his disciples (cf. especially the reference to "mourning" rather than "fasting" in Mt 9:15, and more generally cf. Jn 16:16–20). The two parables which follow contrast sharply the conduct of Jesus disciples with that of John's disciples and the Pharisees (Mk 2:21–22).

Jesus and Fasting in General.

Despite the saying of Mark 2:19–20, elsewhere Jesus appears to take for granted that some fasting will continue during his ministry (Mt 6:16–18). In the Sermon on the Mount he criticizes its ostentatious display. Contrary to the practice of hypocrites, genuine fasting should be conducted toward God alone and disguised toward others by a joyful, even lavish, appearance. Jesus reference to fasting here should not be interpreted as an injunction to fast. It is more a recognition of its congruity with prayer (Mt 6:5–15) and simplicity (Mt 6:19–34) in the lifestyle of his Jewish disciples.

Jesus Experience of Fasting.

Several times Jesus is described as going without food and drink. He does so during his sojourn in the wilderness (*see* Mountain and Wilderness) prior to his temptations (Mt 4:2 and par.; *see* Temptation of Jesus) when he rises early to pray in a solitary location (Mk 1:35) and as a result of his ministering to those in need (Mk 8:31). On one occasion he declared to his disciples that he had "food" to eat of which they were ignorant, so referring to his fulfillment of his Father's purpose (Jn 4:31–34). Such passages suggest that for Jesus fasting was often a corollary of other activities to which he gave a high priority—spiritual struggle, prayer and evangelism. He does not take up fasting as a discipline in its own right.

There is no evidence that he fasted regularly during the time of his public ministry. His concern that he and his disciples gain sufficient sustenance after extending themselves for other's sake (Mk 2:23) and that people coming to hear him who had missed out on a meal be properly fed (Mk 8:1–13) are also revealing. So too are his associating hospitality with a person's embracing the good news of the kingdom (Lk 19:5–8; see Kingdom of God) and with both his and his disciple's anticipation of the quality of life in the kingdom itself (Lk 22:14–18; see Table Fellowship).

Fasting in the Early Church.

In line with the secondary place accorded fasting by Jesus, the Apostolic Fathers fail to cite any saying or action of Jesus as a justification of fasting as a religious discipline. Though other references to fasting occur on Jesus lips (Mk 9:29; Mt 17:21), textual critics are now satisfied that this is due to an early gloss. Such additions also exist outside the gospels and indicate the importance of fasting among some early Christians (Acts 10:30; 1 Cor 7:5). Even so, with the New Testament epistles there is no reference to fasting among Gentile Christians, not even in passages where ascetic practices are mentioned (e.g., Col 2:15–22). However, Jewish Christians, Paul among them, when enduring physical deprivation (e.g., 2 Cor 6:5; 11:27) or engaging in specific prayer (e.g. Acts 13:3; 14:23) seem to have engaged in fasting as it is found in the Old Testament.

Reasons for Fasting from an Article in "Presbyterians Today," by Victor Parachin

1. Like Esther (Esther 4:13-17) – to prepare to meet a challenge

2. To save money from eating out in order to give to a ministry or mission

3. To save time to pray – give up lunch to spend time praying. Can be combined with #2.

4. A reminder that we do not live by bread alone (Mat. 4:4; Deut. 8:3)

5. "An overloaded stomach can interfere with prayer by making us feel sluggish and tired." ~Dr. Hellmut Lutzner.

6. Discipline of our appetites. (#4 reprise)

Reasons for Fasting from *Celebration of Discipline*, by Richard Foster

- To focus and center our attention on God and spiritual things.
- It reveals the things that control us.
- That we do not live by bread alone. (Matthew 4:4)
- Helps us keep balance in life. (1 Corinthians 6:12)
- Discipline brings freedom.

Getting Started for Beginners

❑ Start small. Choose one favorite type of food or drink, or one meal, or one day of the week and limit what you eat on that day. Or it can be a fast from a television program or some other routine that will get your attention by skipping.

❑ Write down what you are fasting from and set a reasonable amount of time to fast. Some examples:

  ❑ Eliminate chocolate from your diet for one month

  ❑ Skip lunch one day a week for two months

  ❑ Eat half your normal portions of all food for one month

  ❑ Limit dessert to one time a week for six weeks

  ❑ Skip news one day a week or a favorite television program for several weeks

❑ Substitute a spiritual "diet" in each of these place. For example, corresponding to the four examples above:

  ❑ Every time you are offered or crave chocolate find a way to take a few minutes to pray or read scripture or journal about your fasting experience

  ❑ During this lunch time mediate on a passage of scripture, journal about what you are experiencing in your spiritual life, begin a prayer journal and use this time to record prayers and any answers, practice lectio and listening

  ❑ Every day you limit your portions set aside some time to read and meditate on scripture, journal about your spiritual experiences, or spend time praying, or practice *lectio divina* and listening

  ❑ The days you eliminate dessert set aside time to pray, meditate, or journal

  ❑ Use the normal news time or television time to read and meditate on scripture or pray

Acknowledgments

I am especially thankful to my congregation, San Clemente Presbyterian Church, that provided much of the platform for developing *Groundings*. I am grateful for two pastors and colleagues, Steve Wright and Craig Williams, who sat down with me at the very beginning to brainstorm and flesh out my ideas. I am thankful to the more than one hundred people at San Clemente Presbyterian who entrusted their sacred lives of faith to this experience. I am especially thankful to Sheryl France-Moran, a coworker and beloved friend at San Clemente Presbyterian Church, and one of the first students who enthusiastically embraced and lived out *Groundings* and is now teaching the experience to others. In addition, as Mission Participation Director she has worked with me to incorporate the *Groundings* principles in the orientation and execution of all our mission teams. It has made a difference in the way these teams approach going into the world.

I am thankful for my husband Drew who always provides the space and support for me to pursue whatever it is I believe God is calling me to do. Even if it means being on his own foraging for food in the refrigerator, or my absence for days and weeks at a time, seeing me up late at night, up early in the morning, and sometimes, up all night; he cheers me on with a steady, "Go for it Candie, but pace yourself." I always need both the encouragement and the caution.

Finally, I am thankful to the Lord for all of the grace and patience extended to me on this journey to follow Him and drag others along with me. A poor and very ordinary young girl, I have had the rich privilege of serving Christ in extraordinary places and times in extraordinary ways. And because it has helped me to see the extraordinary work of God in ordinary places, I consider the *Groundings Experience* to be one of the richest privileges of all. To God be the glory.

About the Author

Candie Blankman has been in ministry more than thirty years and an ordained Presbyterian pastor since1996. Candie serves as Pastor of Discipleship, Care, and Engagement at San Clemente Presbyterian Church. Candie has also been a junior and senior high school teacher, a restaurant manager, and has spoken at retreats and conferences for many years. She has been a presenter and coach for SCORRE Speaker Training since 1985. However, Candie's passion is studying the Bible and then teaching and preaching it in a way that reveals the living and powerful Christ.

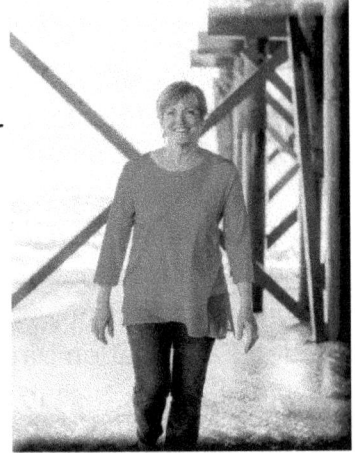

In 2013 Candie began developing Groundings as a foundational discipleship experience designed to transform the often-complacent church culture from one of knowing about Jesus, to one that is following the living Christ into the world. Through five Jesus narratives, Groundings inspires participants to experience discipleship and evangelism as a seamless garment.

When spare time shows up, she walks the beach and writes and paints. She has been married for 42 years to Drew, senior copy editor for InterVarsity Press, and together they have raised three children—this is where she has learned the most about being a minister. Now her five grandchildren are teaching her even more.